THERE IS SOMETHING LESS

AYAN BHAR

Made with ♥ on the Notion Press Platform
www.notionpress.com

To my family and friends.

Contents

Preface   *ix*

Songs Of Love & Heartbreak

1. Ghost Of You   3

2. Aarohi, Must You Remain The Girl   5

3. Aarohi, You Were My First Poem   6

4. To Aarohi   7

5. Aarohi, My Heart's Remembering You   8

6. Aarohi, Be Close To Me   9

7. If My Dreams Could Have Been True   10

8. Aarohi   12

9. Aarohi, Oh Your Eyes!   13

10. If I Meet You One Day   14

11. There Is Something Less   17

12. Ten Parts Of Beauty Came Down   20

13. Another Life   21

14. Aarohi, Put Your Hand On My Heart   23

15. Old Soul   24

16. The First Time We Met   26

17. Daydreaming   27

18. Aarohi, Be That Love   28

19. Aarohi, You Are Too Beautiful   29

20. Aarohi, Now To Think Of You   30

21. Aarohi, The Stars Are Getting Dim   31

22. Aarohi, Still I Love You   33

Contents

23. Remember Me If You Get Some Time   34

24. Till My Heart Breaks Apart   35

25. Aarohi, If You Stayed   36

26. Aarohi, To Have Loved You   37

27. Aarohi, How Far You Are   38

28. Fallen Leaf   39

29. Aarohi, Your Endless Eyes   40

30. The Time's Passing By   41

31. You Must Remember What You Did To Him   42

32. There Is Something More   44

Songs Of Introspection & Observation

33. Insignificant   47

34. Kolkata 2023   48

35. Winter Has Came   50

36. A Sonnet For My Younger Self   53

37. WB Yeats   54

38. Transcreation Of A Song Of Tagore   55

39. Listen   56

40. Dawn Breaks By The Riverlet   57

41. Here Lies A Silence   58

42. Hesperus   59

43. Madness Of Man   60

44. The Golden Deer   61

45. The Drinking Song   63

Contents

46. October 2024 — 64

47. You Are A Miracle — 65

48. Kolkata 2024 — 68

49. The Butchers — 70

50. The Mouse Trap — 71

51. The Rage Of Nrisingha — 73

52. Requiescat: To A Dead Lover — 75

53. Someone — 76

54. Whatever I Have Written — 78

Preface

I have gathered most of the poems I have written in the last two years and decided to publish them. This book is divided into two parts — *Songs of Love & Heartbreak* and *Songs of Introspection and Observation.*

The first section, *Songs of Love & Heartbreak*, chronicles the ebbs and flows of love and dreams. I can't write poetry on my own, if I want to write a single line I can't. But when the tremendous chaos of dreams stricken my mind, they sometimes harmoniously fall under a rhythm, only then I try to collect verses out of them. But most of the time when they don't, and remain inextricably inter-tangled amongst themselves, my mind suffocates.

The *Songs of Love & Heartbreak* may seem centered on a single muse — **Aarohi**, a name that recurs like a refrain, is not just a woman, rather she is all the women I have loved at some point in time — she represents love in myriad forms. I fell in love with Aarohi many many times, in many many lifetimes — sometimes she is my first girlfriend, sometimes she is the girl I secretly used to like, sometimes she is my college crush, sometimes she is the girl who broke my heart — and she is the same girl I fell in love with in Florence five hundred years ago, or in Babylon four thousand years ago — she is the girl who has maddened and troubled my wandering soul for ages!

The second section, *Songs of Introspection and Observation*, reflects on life, philosophy, the passage of time, and the world's fleeting beauty. Burdened with the visions of history and mankind's spirit, I write lines troubled with the essence of existence and the mysteries that surround us.

Ayan Bhar

24/01/2025

Songs of Love & Heartbreak

1. Ghost of You

You come to my mind still,
Tho' many moons have gone,
Many a dew-dabbled dawn,
Salty waves from hill to hill.

You come to me like dreams,
Dew-drenched petals of rose,
Drizzle-hazy horizon compose
Colours in a fairy bow it seems.

Your sway before my weary eyes,
Your face has not changed at all,
I remember you from our last fall,
Old stars shiver in changing skies.

You go from half-awaken eyes,
When the streets' cacophony
And chaos suddenly shakes me,
The crowd goes on and cries.

I have surrendered to this curse —
Like the night is twined with day
And darkness with the starry way,

You must be the muse of my verse.

My heart must burn in blazing blue,
I must carry the ghost of you.
Under the dreams dropping like dew,
I must carry the ghost of you.

2. Aarohi, Must You Remain the Girl

Aarohi, do not hold his hands, do not go with him,
Must you remain the girl I loved for myriad times,
Must you remain the girl of ancient love rhymes,
Must your sparkling cervine eyes not get dim!

Must you trouble the hearts of men in youth,
Their drowsy eyes in sleepless nights must cry
Just to drown in your oceanic hair, and die;
For that is all worth for life and love and truth!

3. Aarohi, You were My First Poem

Somewhere in the crowd of dreams
You were my first poem out of whims
Of my dream-delighted teen heart
(That was once indifferent to art
And wasted verses once did seem)
Suddenly started to daydream
A crowd of verses like fireflies
Just to praise your glistening eyes.

And from then I live but write
For the coming poets must know
The star-stitched sky of night
And my gladdened heart did bow
Before your eyes drenched with light
Like winter's sun-sparkling snow.

4. To Aarohi

I have seen stars to burn, and my heart too,
Like on midsummer's night I have seen you
And hold you in my arms tight, and said,
Upon my warm chest keep your head
And hold your tongue dear, words are waste,
Let the eyes speak and the hearts rest!

Did not at that night your eyes seem to me
The most precious thing I had ever come to see?
And then I went on walking on the moonlit shore,
Picked up pearl-shells to find a pearl that is more
Beautiful than your eyes, and gazed at the sky
To find a star more beautiful than your eye —

But nah! Not a single pearl by the phosphorus sea
Nor a star of the star-crowed sky seemed to me
So beautiful as your eyes! And I never will find
Anything that will tremble and madden my mind
Like your eyes do. The waves went on lamenting away,
The stars dimmed, and the mournful sky faded to grey.

5. Aarohi, My Heart's Remembering You

When the dusk comes suddenly
The southern sky dims,
Oh! my heart's remembering you
And all of your whims.

Your long kohl-black waving hairs,
Your eyes and boundless smile,
Oh! banish me from this indifferent life
And let us go to a secluded exile!

I etch your name by the star-thrones
And write your beauty in rhyme,
Oh! the posterity must remember you
Until the end of endless time.

6. Aarohi, Be Close to Me

I drowned in burning stars, the lights' cacophony
Riddled my eyes; I have seen wonders of universe,
I carry burdens of knowledge — an ancient curse,
Aarohi, you please be more close, close to me.

Let the sky get dark, let the stars burn and fall,
The ancient kings may rest in the yellow pages,
So the words of old prophets and wise sages,
Aarohi, you please be more real, real than all.

I went on asking each dewdrop and pearl-shell
Where have you been, please come and tell
That you won't go anywhere else, just dwell
With me, and let me rest, I am weary as hell!

7. If My Dreams Could Have Been True

If my dreams could have been true the Aegean Sea would wet my heart,

The orange-scented Mediterranean breeze would shake my window,

I would walk on the streets of Greece and meet Plato to talk about art

and philosophy, would talk about the things history does not know.

I would have found you there, and then I would have walked with you

From the streets of Greece to an evening in Florence, we would see

How Da Vinci gave life to the lips of the Mona Lisa and how he drew

Her enchanting eyes; we'd see Kepler staring at the sky sitting by a tree;

We would see Galelio carving his optic glasses under a candlelight;

If my dreams could have been true, you would have been mine,

If my dreams could have been true, then my every lonely night

And day wouldn't have been spent writing many a saddening line!

8. Aarohi

Oh! Aarohi! Whose hands are you holding?
And talking and talking day out and day in!
And smiling by with such sparkling eyes!
The world has grown under changing skies,
Daffodils have grown all over the graveyard
Where the kings and queens sleep unstirred.
The world has grown as my heart old and grey,
Babylon is dust, Assyria has swept away.

Remember, Aarohi, you were a beautiful lass,
Put a pale blue starry pearl in my wine glass
Form your necklace, put your hand on my chest
And said, *"Keep your head upon my breast,
And please love me like tomorrow I will die."*
A star like that blue pearl still shines in the sky.

9. Aarohi, Oh Your Eyes!

Aarohi, oh your eyes! Like the burning stars!
Which far untrodden nebulous ways do you dwell?
They all are dead the kings and sultans and czars,
So the prophets and preachers of heaven and hell,
Still you tread thro' the Milky Way amidst the stars!

Aarohi, I did love you one day,
Still my heart bears your sigh,
I wait like Penelope night and day,
I wait gazing at the giant sky;
My heart's been old and weary and grey!

Aarohi, still I wander in dream-drunken ways,
I wander like a cursed soul like Odysseus,
I wander like a sinful soul like the scripture says
Waiting for judgment from somebody beyond us;
My soul may wander many more nights and days,
Until then upon the dew-dropping cold grass
Let my weary body rest beneath the starry ways.

10. If I Meet You One Day

When many years will have passed
If I meet you one day
Under the falling darkness of May
Like we used to meet
But that time on a different street
In a different place,
Will you be the same? Will your face
Have that magic that you used to have once?
Or the dark shadows will dim your eyes?
When years will have passed if by chance
Under the same stars in changing skies
I will meet you one day
Will you have something to say?

When many years will have passed between us,
Will you have those eyelids like petals of lotus
That used to shine with star-soaked lights
Amidst my darkest nights?
Or will shadows garner in your face?
Will you have that grace
That once maddened many men?
Or that will be lost, will be fallen

From your face as years will have passed!

Will I be the same?
Will I find rhyme
In the breeze, stars, ripples, and sky?
Or as everything gets washed with time
I won't see things through my eye
As I used to see them before
In the days of yore!
The cold stings of time will hurt
My barren heart,
Will I find warmth if I try to search
Other than your cwtch?
How I used to be so insane,
Used to take life as a game,
Won't I be the same?
Years after if we meet again!

Will I feel something, will I?
If we meet years after someday,
"All the days bygone" — if you ask me —
"Is just another leaf fallen from the tree?"
Will I deny?
Or would I say,
"Everything gets washed with time
And the memories are grime
Upon our heart, that too must get washed

As the years will have passed,
Things remain the same no more
Like the days of yore!"
I would say this, wouldn't I?
Or will it be just another lie?

11. There is Something Less

The stars, the fields, the river,

Drizzle-drenched horizon far,

Kingfisher's blue feather

Fallen upon the muddy pond, a star

To a farther star, shivering, dim,

A dream to a farther dream,

Van Gogh is drawing another night,

A sky full of stars bright,

The brown withered broken tree,

The dull darkness, the bats' cacophony,

The owl's glimmering eyes,

The crickets' brawling cries,

Oh my heart! drunk on this wilderness,

These stars, these fields, this dull darkness!

One day she came to me, the same stars were shining,

Upon the boughs of cotton tree the brown starling

Was sweeping weariness from his feathers,

When she came to me, didn't the face of hers

Resemble to the great constellation of heavens?

To the sky of ancient stars? Her eyes

Were pellucid like the eyes of ravens;

O conch-pale stars, come together like fireflies,
Get dream-drunken with her vernal wilderness!

One day when she came to me
And took me amidst the celestial symphony,
And showed me such marvellous sights —
The burning nebulous lights,
A spaceship burned in the white fire,
The broken pieces of it did hurtle and gyre
Round and round and became ashes grey,
Lost somewhere in the Milky Way!

And then she held my hand,
And at last showed me this land,
These fields, these streets, this river,
She showed me winter, Earth was in a deep fever,
Snake sloughs, yellow leaves upon dust,
Cloud-pale mists, dullness and dearth,
The ache-wet heart of the lonely starling,
The burned house, the broken fences, the rust.
She kissed the wind, kissed the Earth,
And then it all was spring!

And now when she is gone
There is something less
In the wind, the stars, the dawn,
In the paddy fields, the wilderness,

I still long for her
Eyes like a burning star,
Her mist-white breasts, her lips
Loving like a dew-drop slowly drips,
Her fairy-embroidered dress;
Now there is something less
In my heart, as she is gone
Upon silvery waves like a swan
I gaze at the monstrous sky
And I sigh.

12. Ten parts of beauty came down

Ten parts of beauty came down
From the heavens furled,
Nine parts were what she got
And the rest to the world.

13. Another Life

I will meet you again when we are fourteen
We will fall in love again like we did,
We will be the same as we have been,
You will hold my hand amid
The falling darkness of April,
And looking at the stars I will wish
To have you forever, to have you until
My mortal body gets burned, or my heart will
Broken apart; we will kiss,
The stars will shine still.

We will fall in love again when we meet,
I will find you, as I have found you many times,
I have walked thro' Babylon and Athens on my feet,
I have sung songs, I have written rhymes
For you for ages; I have seen stars with my naked eye
Thousands of stars spread in the Egyptian sky,
I have seen wars, hundreds of men died,
Their women and mothers cried,
And I have seen you, then have seen no face so fair—
Dream-pastled eyes, pink-faded lips, cascading hair!

But I have lost you in every life, and I will again,

You will break my heart as you did dear,
That's my fate, that's my fate, that's my fate,
You will love me and then you will hate,
You will throw the broken pieces of my heart far,
I will be lost in your life like tears in the rain.

But I will meet you in another life, I will wait
To love you and lose you — that's my fate!

14. Aarohi, Put Your Hand on My Heart

Far somewhere a bonfire is burning red,
Out of the dry leaves of late autumn,
A few hats, a few guns, bottles of rum
Here and there, nostalgia in head,
Stories of old days, stories of boyhood;
A dead cold body of deer, a red hole
Upon her breast, that side of the knoll
She was running in joy across the wood.
Cigarette ashes upon fallen leaves of Pine,
And her cold heart upon burning flame red.
Smell of innocent flesh and blood is spread
Beneath the mighty stars shine.

Put your hand on my heart
It is too heavy, too weary,
The sky's getting dark pitch-dirt,
The half-burned clouds are eerie.
Sit close to me, my heart has
A monsoon of feelings to tell,
But a drop is yet to be dripped, alas!
Warm my heart dear, it is too unwell.

15. Old Soul

As the sun has drowned low
Darkness thickens by my window,
The things I have always wanted to know
I try to think of them in this twilight.
Thoughts swirl in my head, visions run in front of my sight,
What that boy saw when he was coming back home
When darkness was falling on the streets of Rome
The same darkness that has garnered by my window,
That boy saw the birds coming back to their nest,
The dimming lights in the west,
A child in the lap of a young mother,
Golden ripples in the dark waves of Tiber,
A bearded man on an evening roam,
That boy stood a moment, the whole City of Rome
Was stood in front of his eyes still!
Maybe I was that boy — my heart does feel
I have seen everything — I heard the old man's song
About the young days of life, the streets of Rome, I truly belong
To the wheat fields spread up to where the blue met the green
And here I am, thousands of years have passed in between!

Maybe I have been born by the Tiber before by the Ganges,

I think of them — the white palace, giant red curtains, silver glasses
Brimmed with Roman wine; there were jewels, ivories,
An Atrium full of royals and riches, walls full of tapestries,
Fountains in peristyles, white pigeons in cages of gold,
There were so many things forgotten or untold —
There were girls wheatish and fair,
I loved someone among them — who had brown eyes and brunette hair,
Red colours on her nails, flowers in bun, her beauty ages like wine
In my heart even after thousands of years — her eyes shine
Still in my heart like the ancient stars in the Milky Way!
I held her warm naked hands one day,
Put my head on her breast, listened to the beatings of her heart,
Still I hear her heart thousands of years apart!

16. The First Time We Met

The first time we met after coming to this college,
I did feel something for you, a thunderous jolt
Of stormy gust wended in my heart, a mere gaze
Of your eyes shook my old weary heart to moult
Its old withered feathers to feel the world anew!
So I knew — it is a matter of time — I knew —
Before this subtle fascination you rooted deep
Down in my wondering heart, sink down into
The darkest corners of my soul that were asleep,
Cold, dull, sick, and tremble me so hard to and fro
I won't be the same; it's just some time to spend
Before you sink down into my marrows and blend
Your soul with mine! It's just a matter of time
Before this fascination turns in my heart's core
Into something so wild, that I'll question in rhyme
Had I ever truly been in love before?

17. Daydreaming

The professor is writing something on board
From some old yellow pages of a book,
Some are yawning, some are bored,
But here I am daydreaming about you
That is how my life will look
If somehow we end up in the wedding shoe!

We may spend our life far across in some island,
The coconut-scented breeze will kiss our face,
We'll run holding hands on the salt-soaked sand
When Phosphorus-lighten waves will kiss our feet,
And under the shimmering moon we will embrace
Each other so close that in sync our hearts will beat!

18. Aarohi, Be That Love

If you come as the stormy wind wild and free
I will be the leaves of the wood-apple tree,
Will be blown away with you, will twirl and spin
In an ecstatic waltz, amidst the blue and green.

If you come as the huntress in my moonlit glade
I will be the wild deer roaming around unafraid,
Will embrace the death when my chest will bleed
In the love's battlefield, my heart will concede.

Come to me as the wildest night of tempest
When I will sail my ship to the darkening west,
Let the ocean roar and the thunders dance,
Wrap me in chaos, in your cacophonic trance.

But if you ever come as the spring full of love
I will fly in your vibrant sky like a soaring dove,
Will be lost, like I used to get lost in your eyes deep,
Be that love, and let my weary heart fall asleep.

19. Aarohi, You are too Beautiful

You are too beautiful to be touched by my pale hands.
I am one of the shells lying by the sea upon cold sands,
And you are one of the stars glimmering up there in the sky.
I am too mortal to hold you in my hands, even if I cry
For you my screams get lost in the roars of the vast sea
Way before reaching you; this dull world, all this cacophony
Is mine! I am too pale to be yours, too dim to be yours.
Shine, shine high in the sky; I here rest by the sea roars.

20. Aarohi, Now to Think of You

Another's. She will be another's. As she was before my kisses.
- Pablo Neruda.

Now to think of you gazing into his eyes
And kissing his lips uttering words of love
Is killing me inside. How am I supposed to heal?
Now to think of that until the sun dies
Beneath the same stars shivering above
He will have your love that I always wanted to feel
Is killing me inside. Now I feel my sighs
Cold like mist-moist feathers of dove,
Aarohi, how am I supposed to heal?

21. Aarohi, The Stars are Getting Dim

A monsoon of feelings I wished to tell you,
But couldn't shed a drop; though you knew
My heart's been burned from star to farther star,
Or it was an ancient curse that I must carry,
That loving you must burn me, a deep scar
Upon my wandering soul, oh please! Drown me
In your lotus-leafy eyes, for I may heal my heart,
Though this ancient curse will never depart.

If you were here tonight, my heart would have peace.
My heart is burning like fire, the stars are cold as ice,
So your heart was! The dews moisten the wind,
The moonlit river is silvery like the plumes of a swan,
The old boughs are hanging low, a brown snake is twined,
The wind is cold like the barrel of an assassin's gun.
Till we are under the same sky, till the same starlight drips,
How will I accept that your lips would touch another lips?

And now I long for a deep sleep, I need rest,
As my head never going to lie upon your breast,
Let me get lost upon these grasses, wet and cold;
When the next spring comes, I wish we will meet,

We will be young and bright, nothing grey and old
Must touch us, then my ancient heartache may fleet.
All I have wished may that day be true, or it will be just a
dream,
Till then I sleep, among the fallen leaves; the stars are getting
dim.

22. Aarohi, Still I love You

To sate my thirst for life upon your breast
I want to be blended in your white chest
Like the body blends with the heart.

Life is too short like a fleeting blue flame,
So let me live but only to write your name
On the lotus-petals bloomed from dirt.

Life is too short and so my youth days,
Still I love you, like a fly loves the blaze,
Loving you does burn and hurt.

23. Remember Me If You Get Some time

Let these passionate lines of mine drown
In your sweetest dreams and reveries,
So some fine day if you would sit down
And turns the pages of old memories —
You would find the verses I wrote down.

My soul had wished to have you, even
Knowing that you will never be mine,
Yeats too wished for the cloths of heaven,
Poets are fools, they try to entwine
Dreams and reality time and again.

Remember me if you get some time, remember
How I loved you once, ah! How I loved you!
Each corner of your soul will whisper ear to ear
How I loved you once, ah! How I loved you!

24. Till My Heart Breaks Apart

I tried to draw your dream-pasteled eyes
On the pale canvas of my heart,
I tried to draw those cascading hairs
Out of my life's darkness and dirt,
I tried to draw those pink-faded rose-lips
And gave all of my soul to my art;
But I failed, I failed whenever I tried
And I fail whenever I start.
You are the starry way my body can never touch,
So I failed, I fail whenever I start.
You are the spring my wintry heart can never feel,
So the cold stings of time still hurt.

But I try and try to etch your face
On the pale canvas of my heart,
Till my mortal body gets burned
Or my heart breaks apart.

25. Aarohi, If You Stayed

Sometimes at some idle nights after a tiring day
When I lie in bed, thoughts swirl in my head
That how my life would have been in its way
If you listened to me, thought twice, and stayed.

My whole life would have been spent with you,
The July sky would have been kinder to us,
The old stars might have worn lights anew,
The nights would have been fairyful if we lay on grass
By my village river moistened with the dropping dew.

I would have played with your long black hair,
I wouldn't have been so lonely 'cause my head
Would find your breast to rest in times of despair,
Oh! How my life would have been if you stayed!

26. Aarohi, to have Loved You

To have loved you I have known
The clock's ticking to eternity,
To have loved you I've been lone
In the crowdest morns of my city.

To have loved you I've understood
Though how much for you I yearn,
Like a fly amidst the flaming wood
My heart in your love too must burn.

27. Aarohi, How Far You Are

You are a distant island, adorned in blossoms rare,
A land of mystery, with secrets you do not share.
And I, a humble bee, charmed by your sweet allure,
Forever seeking your nectar, forever longing for more.
I want to get bathed in the colours of your spring,
And want to fly in your sky where rainbows shine,
Where the vibrant shades of life and love do sing
The songs of joy; I want to drink the golden wine
Out of sun; but I am waiting in this vale of dark
Why don't you come here? And why don't you hark
Our hearts cry? the lone sky fades to the grey
And the barren earth amid this arid winter cry!
You dwell far amidst the untrodden starry way,
Why don't you come here in our dimmed sky?

28. Fallen Leaf

You are the summer's cloud in the west,
Calm and silent, but have fire in heart,
You roar aloud tearing the sky's chest
Shaking all the men on the lumbering cart
Who are heading to plough their lea,
You lighten the whole sky in your glee.

I am one of the leaves amidst dust
Fallen from the wood-apple tree,
Will be blown with your June's gust
And adrift amongst the wind free.
I will fall down upon the boulevard
And get old and brown and hard.

If you come in this way someday under the setting sun
Walk on me, give me the dust of your white naked feet,
As my place isn't amongst those blossoms in your bun,
I am a fallen leaf, you won't take me up from the street;
Those blossoms will shine in the colours of glee
And I am just a brown leaf fallen from the tree.

29. Aarohi, Your Endless Eyes

I love to get lost in those two eyes
To see mysteries of the universe hidden
To see the land of thousands of fireflies
And the dances of my life's joy and pain;
My weary heart wandered in the gloom
Until I have found zillions of stars bloom
Whence — whence all the lights dance
My heart gets rest; what I have found
Those endless eyes of yours by chance
I won't be lost anywhere else around!
Long I have been lost in the world's paths
Over the plains and the hills and straths,
I have searched for you in front of my eye for long
But I failed, as you've been inside my eye all along!

30. The Time's Passing By

Darling, Put on your untidy gown,
The mellow sun is setting down,
The moon is smiling in the sky
Don't let me wait in vain and sigh.
Let those wet curls blow in the air
Let the flowers fall from your hair,
The pearl necklace of your neck
And the golden anklets break,
And let the golden earrings fall
I don't care, I don't care at all!
Let the two weary souls kiss.
Let this be an ephemeral bliss.
The stars are shivering in the sky,
Come soon, the time's passing by.

31. You Must Remember What You Did to Him

Don't you see what you have done to him?
Neath all there was a man who wanted love,
But your fickle heart was a vivacious dove
Flew in the vernal skies and lived on its whim.

Didn't you imagine a perfect man in your dream?
And made a perfect image in your manic mind,
Searched for that man in him but couldn't find,
So you took his soul and crushed it out of him.

Don't you remember what you wanted from him?
Though he brought you a sky full of starry light
You cried for the moon on the new moon's night,
Still he tried to pour light in your soul to the brim.

Don't you know what you have done to him?
There was a man who wanted to be himself,
But you took all the lights of his soul like pelf
And left the man all broken and dull and dim.

Wasn't your love a moment's fleeting gleam?
Wasn't your love a fugacious whimsical wish?

Didn't you throw his heart into a dark abyss?
So you must remember what you did to him.

32. There is something more

There is something more to be told,
Aarohi, come back, oh do not hold
His hands! Do not go with him away!
Must you come back, Aarohi, one day—
Maybe in another life, maybe in another spring,
Under the dreamingly dropping dew
When a cuckoo upon the cotton-tree will sing
I will be a young man again for you!
And again you must break my heart,
For you must be the muse of my art.

Songs of Introspection & Observation

33. Insignificant

The great tapestry is being woven,
Look, look up to the endless sky!
For losing one mere bead you cry?
Look, look up to the starry heaven,
The planets and planetoids are there
Spinning and hurtling in the vast space,
Someone who treads in the starry ways
Is writing a great grand book, you are
Just a mere page, sighing over tiny things.
Look up to the sky, and try to be more
As when you will be gone to the stars' door
There will not be regrets' ghostly wings
To haunt you, and then, when you will look
Back to the road with a sound sigh,
Do you want to see yourself from the sky
As a mere yellow page of that book?

34. Kolkata 2023

I heard that dreamy dews fall here upon every street!
And this is the city of joy, the city of many a dream;
I saw the buildings stand high maybe hundreds of feet
Piercing the sky holding the city's pride and esteem.
I came and went to a mall looking for something to buy
And saw all the people were happy and beautifully clad,
All their sons and daughters had shiny diamond-eye,
Their happy faces make every mother and father glad.
There's love among every lover and husband and wife,
There's a dream in the eyes of every young girl and boy,
And everyone's chasing their dreams, this city is full of life,
And I was fully convinced that this is the City of Joy!

While I was returning I saw something very strange,
Between the sky-high buildings there was dark gloom,
I saw some creatures there that made my mind derange
And who were those creatures I was trying to assume.
Then I saw a man lying there coldly, and a child and a dog
Sharing something out of dirt; the child had eyes iron-red
Glowing like fireballs in the falling darkness and fog,
He crawled towards the man and tried to shake his head
But he didn't wake up, he was sleeping for many a day,
But that child tried still, he will also fall asleep very soon;

The dreamy dews fall here upon every street they say
Or is it the tears of that child shining under the moon?

35. Winter has Came

While I am writing this rhyme
Winter has come to my door
Again for the nineteenth time
With cold memories of yore.

Winter has come again to me
As an old friend who stays
In the times of melancholy
And in the times of hard ways.

Winter has come, the southern wind blows,
Silent are the birds, dry are the woodlands,
The naked trees stand still like scarecrows,
The long fields are empty as a monk's hands.

Winter has come once more
Again for the nineteenth time
Knocking on my room's door
Waking me from my daydream.

I dreamt all my years bygone
And all those people I knew
Flashing in front of me one by one

And getting lost leaving me in blue.

I dreamt a young child was busy to play
With his toys, he drew a house and a tree;
He was young, bright, cheerful and gay,
So he danced around with brimming glee.

I dreamt that child grew old and became me,
Big hairs curled up to the neck,
I dreamt I loved someone who once loved me
Who took my heart only to break.

I dreamt of my old lover's hair
Spreading over my face and lips,
And I dreamt her face — so fair
Serene like a dewdrop slowly drips.

I dreamt my old lover's eyes
Brimmed with star-soaked lights,
Like how the sparkle of fireflies
Fly around amid summer nights.

I dreamt my old lover walked away
And I was alone standing there still,
All the words failed to make her stay
All the words failed to make her feel.

As winter has knocked on my door
My dream must come to an end,
For the nineteenth time I will adore
And greet my sweet old friend!

36. A Sonnet for My Younger Self

If I can go back and meet my version of young
And can gift him some words from my tongue,
I'd give him some learnings that I've learnt late —
To take a sit and breathe and watch and wait
In the times when the mind tangles up in blue,
For he must not see the things that are not true
And are built up in his mind in love or in hate.
I'd forbid to do many things he thinks are right,
As he had not seen yet the brutal hands of fate,
Nor had seen the fool's victory or the evil's sleight;
But I know that his bohemian soul would debate
And would not listen to any of my words, despite
Being warned — a sword is often mightier than ink,
He would go for his whims and what he does think.

37. WB Yeats

When the daffodil-yellow sky dreams under dusk,
The pearl-pale stars slowly dreamingly shimmer,
A man with drowsy eyes and a weary heart writes
Dream-drunken verses remembering someone far.

Sighing man bothered with a fire-heart woman
And her wine-aging beauty tightened as a bow,
Men have burned many Troys for women like her,
And at the end only ashes remain, dews drop slow.

38. Transcreation of a Song of Tagore

If they do not hold up the light
When the storm troubles the night,
If they all close their doors, O forlorn,
O thou ill-fated soul, then ignite
With the thunder flames bright
The ribs of your chest, and walk alone!

39. Listen

When the lights dripping from the stars
Shines on the blue petals of the rose,
And the shadows of untold manuscripts
Unfolds themselves and slowly compose
Their stories with the ripples of Damodar,
Come here, O wayfarer, come here close
Rest a while you weary soul, put your ear
On the heart of the old Banyan, and hear
The stories of yore, the stories no one knows,
Unheard, or forgotten, the days have fallen
Like brown leaves from the tree of time;
Listen quietly, by whence Damodar flows
And the breeze blows with grains of pollen,
Sit on the wet grass, and listen to the rhyme!

40. Dawn Breaks by the Riverlet

Dawn breaks by the riverlet,
Upon the grasses dew-wet
Yesterday-twilight's cow-steps,
Shadowy arboreal shapes,
The mist-moistened Earth,
Starling's heart full of mirth,
Tales of yore, fairies, many a lore,
Someone who came way before
And walked on this street,
Washed his dusty feet
In this pond, he spent his night
Beneath the starry sky bright
Under the old Banyan tree,
With the corvine cacophony
He headed to somewhere else,
That unknown wayfarer's tales
May still be found
Under the noisy sound
Of hurlyburly of day,
His sighs still may
Be heard if one listens carefully
The heart of the old Banyan tree!

41. Here Lies a Silence

Here lies a silence, a melancholy, like the heart
Of dragonflies, like the yellow grasses, muddy dirt,
Like the feathers of the weary raven, a cold
Silence like these is spread onto the fields, the old
Banyan tree's roots are spread, just like that;
Jackles are howling far, curious eyes of a rat
Looking upon the starful sky, a weary solitude
Upon the dusty roads cold and bedewed.

42. Hesperus

Wanna go back to the blue twilights of my townlet,
Loved those calm breezes, birds coming to nest.
The paddy fields and muddy ponds used to wait
For the darkness, the Hesperus shone in the west.

Hands in pocket, curly careless hair, strange mind,
I loved those eves, the carelessness, the wind;
With the craziest thoughts of life and death
I had fiery dreams in my every breath.

43. Madness of Man

There was a young man I knew
Who chased illusions in the mirage,
Ignored all the warnings of peers
And ran after spoilage and sabotage.

Because a young man's blood is hot
Just as midsummer's rebellious sun,
But his heart is crazy and stubborn
Gets maddened by flowers in women's bun.

He dreams of a tyrannical monarch
Where he burns the King in a blaze,
Hoist the flag of revolution and glory,
Walks amidst slogans and praise.
But this brave day-dream-warrior
Often gets defeated by mere women's gaze.

44. The Golden Deer

I was walking thro' woods when the great star was burning in
sky,
I was weak, sweat-drooled, and all of a sudden in front of my
eye
A deer appeared, a golden deer! Its body was as if of pure gold
Shining in daylight like an old king's wealth, What did I
behold!
It was among the leaves, It came here from some lost pages
Of some ancient lores or some mystics of old forgotten ages!

It seemed like it was the highest wealth to have for any man,
All kings' and merchants' golds and diamonds had no worth,
All men's greed converges in it, no jewel is more precious than
That golden deer! The man who hasn't seen it is a vain of birth;
I stood with feelings I can't explain, I couldn't hold myself, I
ran
In joy and delight, out of insanity, out of madness and mirth!

It was in front of my eye, but going far and far, I couldn't get
near,
I cried aloud, I ran with all my strength, but that elusive deer
Was like the horizon that goes back and back as far as one does
go,

I cut myself with thorns, I lost myself, where I was I didn't know,

I was exhausted, and riddled with light and dark, green and brown,

I had no more soul to run, my heart was beating fast, I fell down.

The last thing I remember, I awoke and somehow came out of wood,

The deer was gone, I couldn't find it, but I hoped someday I would.

45. The Drinking Song

O all my friends sit around
And open the bottle of rum,
Let us go then and not get found,
Let us go wild and be like a bum.

Let us pour the warm rum
Into our throats and sing —
Man must live like a bum
Before he becomes a king!

46. October 2024

The sky has lightened up with devilish lights.
Nothing's changed, a century has passed in vain.
The arm-sellers write the books of laws and rights,
What follows but blooded rivers and nuclear rain!

Our old peace preachers' graves shine
With flowers on their birthdays,
Our children beautifully orate many a line
From their poems and essays.

Our old peace preachers' lymph and blood
Now enrich the soil earthworm treads,
Or their ashes have washed in rain-flood,
Or microbes have eaten their big heads.

Some of them might have cried in the past
Amidst their many a speech and song—
"My body will be gone, but my ideas will last."
How we failed them! They all were wrong.

Their books, dusted off, serve to adorn our shelves,
Epetomes of intellect, but are hollow in themselves.

47. You are a Miracle

Have you ever thought my friend that you are a miracle?

Or staring at the stars you have been thinking on the cosmic scale

You are nothing but dust drifting in randomness, leaving behind no trail

When the wind of time will wipe you out, and till then it's all fate —

Haven't you ever thought you are a miracle? Let me tell you my mate,

Don't you think your birth was the most miraculous and meticulous act

By the nature or God or whatever you want to call that doesn't alter the fact

That you are the most habile piece of creation, every event in past —

All the empires, wars, revolts, all the men who fought for power and lust,

All the men who fought for their beliefs, their Gods, heaven, and glory,

All the men who preached peace, all the prophets who told some divine story,

All the men who died in wars, all the rebellions who were punished to death,

All the men who brought revolutions and fought until their last breath,

All the men who built monuments, carved sculptures, painted their canvas,

All the men who ploughed their fields when their goats trod on green grass,

All the men who built swords, knives, axes, whips, gun powders and guns,

All the men who built astronomy, geometry — the Greeks and the Romans,

The Indians, Egyptians, or the Babylonians who looked at the nocturnal sky

To know the world and beyond, to know us, to know what really does lie

Deep inside the heart of darkness; all have done what they could've done,

And all the people of each time have lived their life, all have lost or won

Their wars for wealth or glory, for truth or belief, or just to live a life of peace

All across the globe all across the ages — Rome, Cairo, Babylon, or Greece

All of them who lived by the Nile, Tiber, Indus, Ganges, or the Aegean Sea —

All lived their life in such a way that your ancestors met every time in history!

The whole history of mankind has converged into you, aren't

you a miracle?

What haven't men seen? Famines, pandemics — many men couldn't prevail

Thro' the dark days of life, but your ancestral chain has never been broken,

As if it has been protected by some galactic guardians or forces of heaven!

All those stars shine in the sky, you are one of them, believe me my friend,

You belong to the eternity, to the infinity, to the unknown, you have no end.

48. Kolkata 2024

This city is always in a hurry, always in a rush!
People are running all the time, all the places
Filled with people with sweat-drooled faces;
I was traveling in a suffocating crowded bus,
All the men I saw carried stress in their eyes,
This city is too cruel, too harsh, at least for me;
The air smothered me, the traffic's cacophony
Annoyed my rusty heart! The whole city cries
Like a wandering ghost who died long ago
But appears to live. People on my bus were pale,
The people were very common in a nutshell
Trying to live a life and feed their family, so
They all were, what I think, ignorant about
The fact that some men out there exist
Who are calculating distances of intergalactic
Stars and planets, some men are searching out
How this endless gigantic universe was born.
Will those people on the bus ever going to know
There were men five thousand years ago
Who were just like them? They are long gone,
But how did they look? How did they dream?
I wish to know, to know the things lost in time,
To read a thousand books, and many a rhyme,

Life must not be a moment's fleeting gleam!
But this city is too dull, too broken, too grey,
Just indifferent men feeding their lives every day.

49. The Butchers

The vultures are flying 'round the sky
The wolves and jackals are coming nigh,
The vultures are slowly coming down
And they fight for that golden crown.

Some poets are rhyming their songs,
Having love-nights upon flower-bed;
The hungry child is looking at the sky
As if the moon is a huge burnt bread.

The butchers are running my countryland,
With a claque of thinkers who day and night
Are romanticizing their blood-soaked hand;
The wolves and jackals wear a white shirt
And keep their sharp nails and teeth out of sight,
The truth is in front, who, who will blurt?

50. The Mouse Trap

I was in my room in our house,
I was disturbed by some weird sound,
After looking here and there I found
Something was running around
Under my bed — it was a mouse!

I put a cage at night with a slice of potato in it,
Started to wait on the bed, put on a nice song,
But didn't have to wait for long —
It was brown, mid-sized, and young,
Caught in the cage, raging, didn't want to submit.

I tried to put the cage out of my room with care,
It was trying to bite my fingers, I was a little afraid,
I tried gently taking the cage out from under my bed.
It was squeaking, whirling, trying to bring out its head
And bite my fingers, it really gave me a bit of fear.

I released it in my yard so it can get out of our house,
It quickly ran and disappeared in the cold dark,
I looked in front, felt the breeze, and did hark
The hooting of an owl, croaking of frogs, jackals' bark,
It was a great night, I wished a good night to that mouse.

After coming back I remembered I had forgotten the cage,
It was outside with some leftovers of potato in it and open,
Thought to bring it back the next day, put some songs again,
Tried to fall asleep after all day's work with a weary brain,
Thinking about that mouse, it was cute but full of rage.

When I went to bring that cage back the next day
That same mouse was trapped in that same cage,
Again squeaking, whirling, trying to escape, full of rage,
What was that? Stupidity? Greed? Insanity of young age?
Can someone trap himself in the same cage in the same way?

51. The Rage of Nrisingha

Hiranyakashipu was the fierce demon-king,
When he conquered all the earth and heaven
It was forbidden to utter and worship or sing
Gods' names, or else your head would be cloven!
Lord Vishnu, as his fourth avatar came
Listening to the prayers of demon-prince
Pralhada, the devotee, taking the lord's name
He cried, *"O Lord! If thou dost exist, evince
Thyself in this hour of need!"* Then his Lord
Came as the human-body with lion-head
(As demon-king was blessed that no sword
Or weapon or man or animal can even dread
Him, nor kill him, nor he'd defeated in the day
Or at night, nor inside his house or outside).
Like a monstrous creature looking for prey.
Even feared by him the sun went to hide,
In the right hour of twilight, nor day or night
Nrisingha, the ferocious avatar, did roar.
Hiranyakashipu couldn't even give a little fight,
Nrisingha, sitting on the threshold of palace-door
Placed the king on his lap and severed his chest
With his sharp claws! And then all evils fled.
And the words of the coming of God spread

To everywhere from the East to the West.

52. Requiescat: To a Dead Lover

Now it feels strange that you are not here,
It's hard to explain how I feel, I feel gloom
And I feel a strange emptiness in my room;
I owe you many things — your love and care
And your wisdom, I feel blessed I had you.
I wish you eternal joy for your journey ahead
Beyond our faded dreary world and spread
Amongst the stars way above our sky's blue.
Will forget you one day, all the promises are lie
The promises to remember someone for long,
Many lovers will come, and you'll be lost among
Old sweet memories as the time will pass by.
But I am glad, glad that I had you in my way,
And I wish to find someone like you one day.

53. Someone

I saw her standing there
Among the crowd's flood,
Never seen a face so fair
Like a lotus amidst mud.

I did want to yell
"O girl! Who're you?
Where do you dwell
With such eyes blue!

How you've got that face
Serene like falling dew
From heavens with grace!
I wanted to ask you.

How can I believe my eye
That you are false or true?!
Under the same blue sky
How someone lives like you!

I want to see you close —
Those curls of golden hue,
Those lips seemed like rose

From the distance I see you.

But I am one of the throng
I'd not get noticed I knew,
In the mud truly I belong
Not a lotus like you!"

I did want to yell aloud
"O girl! Give me time few
Tho' I belong to the crowd
But I want to see you!"

I tried to gather strength to yell
"O girl! I want to see you,
How beautiful you're I want to tell!"
But she gave a sudden adieu.

I lost her amidst the crowd,
She must've gone to her fairyland —
Under the sea or upon the cloud;
So I stood here head in hand.

I saw her standing right there
Or 'twas a dream I don't know,
But that face — still I remember
In my moments of joy and woe.

54. Whatever I have Written

Take only the drunkness out of my every line
And drown your eyes with dream-secreted wine.
Whatever I have written so far, it must seem
Drunk words of a maddened man lost in a dream.
O beautiful reading soul, sitting far from me in time,
Must you not get wised but get drunk with my rhyme!

Thank You

Contact the Author

Gmail: ayanbhar1729@gmail.com

Instagram: ayan_bhar_1

www.ingramcontent.com/pod-product-compliance
Lightning Source LLC
Chambersburg PA
CBHW061438160726
47995CB00003B/942